A TIGER CUB GROWS UP

by Joan Hewett
photographs by Richard Hewett

CAROLRHODA BOOKS, INC./MINNEAPOLIS

IN THE NURSERY

Tara is a tiger cub.

She was born in a wild animal park.

The cub is hungry.

She feels the tip of the bottle.

She drinks her warm milk.

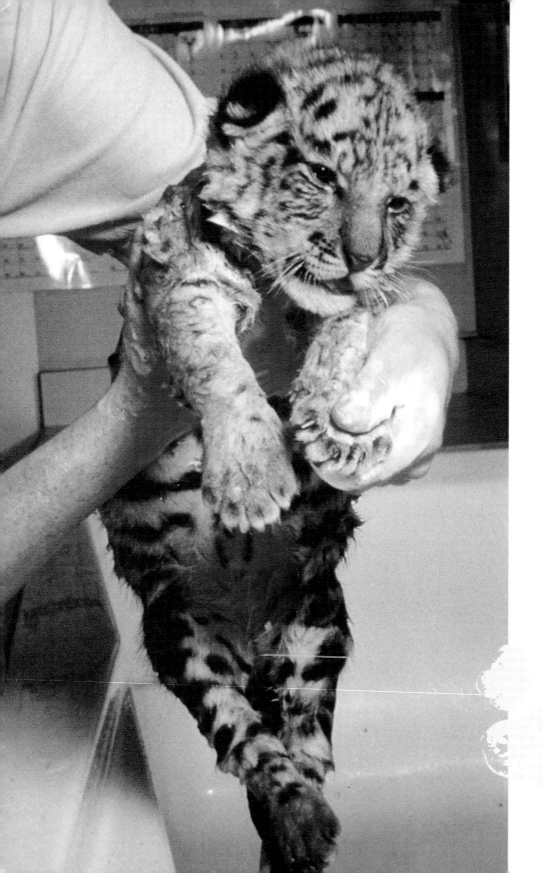

When Tara is
9 days old,
her eyes open.

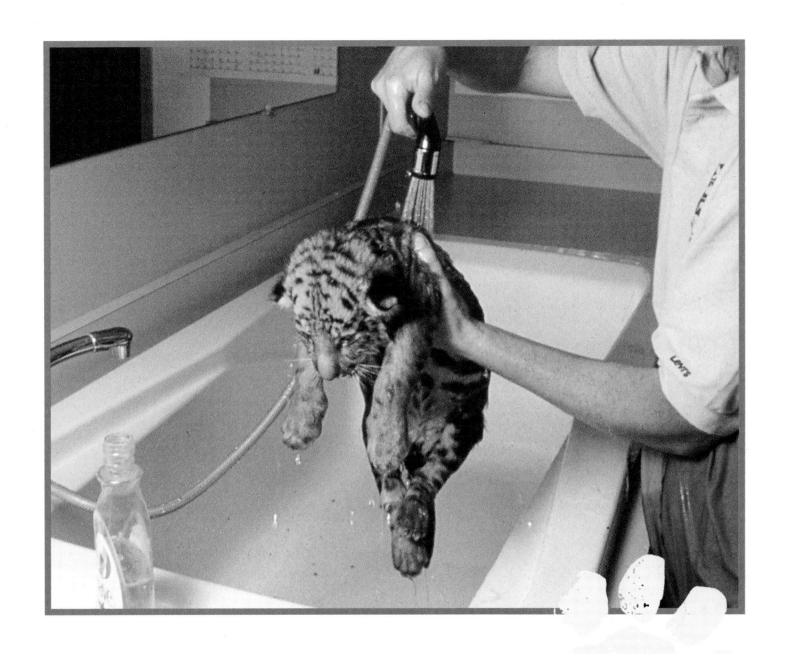

Grown-up tigers like to swim.

But little Tara does not like her first bath.

Mary feeds Tara.

She talks to the tiger cub.

She gives her kisses.

At night, Mary takes the cub home with her.
Tara drinks her milk.
She falls asleep.

Then Tara wakes up.
She is hungry!
She wants more milk.

Tara drinks until her belly is full.
She falls back to sleep.
As she sleeps,
she grunts and squeals.

Tara is 3 weeks old.

Her baby teeth are coming in.

She has pointed teeth for tearing meat.

And she has rounded teeth for chewing.

Chewing feels good.
But a plastic tray is hard to hold
with chubby paws.

Each day, Mary shows the cub a piece of meat.
Tara does not want to try it.
Not yet!

Playtime is a time to learn.

Can Tara crawl over Mary's legs?

How hard will Mary let her bite?

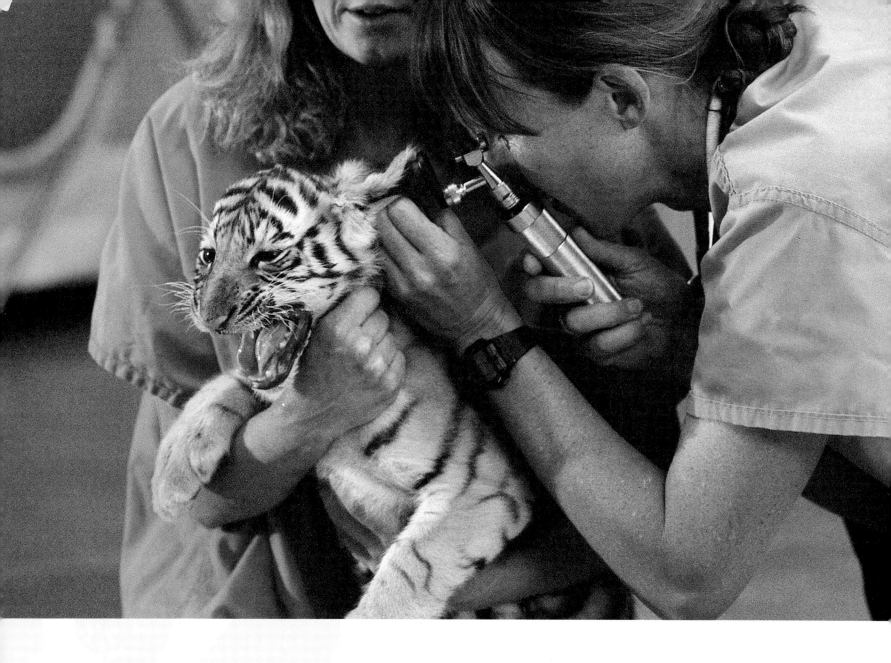

Tara is 3 months old.

Mary takes Tara to the animal doctor.

It is time for a checkup.

The bright lights are scary.
The tiger cub roars.

H-O-W-R-R

Tara is healthy.

And she is old enough to play outside.

TARA GOES OUTDOORS

Grass and sky seem strange to Tara.

The air is filled with new smells.

The tiger cub follows her nose.
She runs across the grass.

Lynn takes care of Tara now.

Lynn hugs Tara.

She plays with Tara.

She shows her falling leaves.

Lynn plays with Tara every day.

She teaches Tara what she can do.

She teaches Tara what she cannot do.

Tara greets Lynn with a friendly chuffing sound.
Lynn returns the greeting.

Climbing over Lynn is fun.

Following Lynn is fun.

Tara creeps along the ground.

Then she pounces!

TARA JOINS THE GROWN-UP TIGERS

Tara is 9 months old.

She is big and strong.

She can join the park's grown-up tigers.

Tara likes her new home.
She can run across the grass.
She can climb on logs.
She can nap under leafy trees.

Tara watches the big tigers swim.

She walks around the pond.

It is hot.

So Tara jumps in.

S-P-L-A-S-H

Tara is 1 year old.

The tiger cub has grown up.

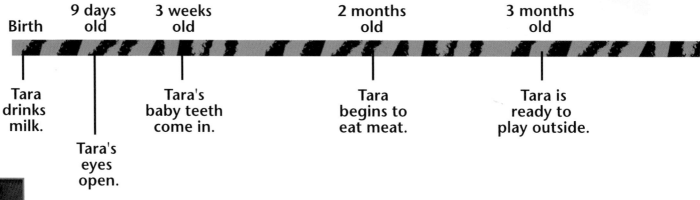

Birth	9 days old	3 weeks old		2 months old		3 months old

Tara drinks milk.

Tara's eyes open.

Tara's baby teeth come in.

Tara begins to eat meat.

Tara is ready to play outside.

More about Tigers

Tigers are wild animals. They are members of the cat family.

Tigers spend most of their time hunting. Each tiger hunts alone. Each has its own hunting ground. One tiger's hunting ground may be larger than a large town.

Tigers are huge. But they are hard to see in the forest. Their amber-brown and black stripes blend with the shadows of trees. Tigers have big padded feet. Their feet help them silently stalk their prey.

Tara is a Bengal tiger. Most Bengal tigers live in the junglelike forests of India. But the forests are disappearing. People are cutting them down to make room for farms and houses. Bengal tigers no longer have room to live and hunt. So tigers have become endangered.

To protect the big cats, India has turned some forests into tiger refuges. India also forbids the sale of wild tigers. Even so, there may not be enough Bengal tigers for them to breed and survive.

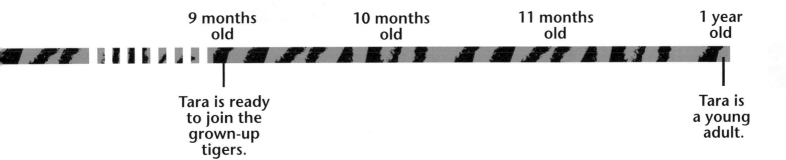

| 9 months old | 10 months old | 11 months old | 1 year old |

Tara is ready to join the grown-up tigers.

Tara is a young adult.

More about Wild Animal Parks

Many zoos and wild animal parks breed captive Bengal tigers. One day, some of these tigers may be returned to the wild.

Tara lives in a wild animal park in northern California. It is called Six Flags Marine World. Between 10 and 14 tigers live here.

Like Tara, the other tigers were born in the park. They have been raised by trainers. The tigers don't need to hunt. But they need exercise. Playing and romping with their trainers keeps them active and healthy.

Tigers can be trained to do what people want them to do. But tigers cannot be tamed. After all, tigers are wild animals. They should never be kept as pets. Still, we are lucky. A visit to a zoo or wild animal park gives us a chance to see these splendid, powerful cats.

To Orson Ridgely Hewett, our first grandchild

This book is available in two editions:
Library binding by Carolrhoda Books, Inc.,
  a division of Lerner Publishing Group
Soft cover by First Avenue Editions,
  an imprint of Lerner Publishing Group
241 First Avenue North
Minneapolis, MN 55401 U.S.A.

Website address: www.lernerbooks.com

Library of Congress Cataloging-in-Publication Data

Hewett, Joan.
  A tiger cub grows up / by Joan Hewett; photographs by Richard Hewett.
    p.   cm.
   ISBN 1-57505-163-X (lib. bdg. : alk. paper)
   ISBN 0-8225-0089-2 (pbk. : alk. paper)
   1. Tiger cubs—Juvenile literature. [1. Tigers. 2. Animals—Infancy.]
I. Hewett, Richard, ill. II. Title.
  QL737.C23 H49 2002
  599.756—dc21   00-011447

Manufactured in the United States of America
2 3 4 5 6 – JR – 07 06 05 04 03 02